P9-DHP-614

BRIAN-

Turn
the
Page

Steve

:)

Turn
the
Page

*A Guide to Moving On
& Letting Go*

STEVE GILLILAND

PEARHOUSE
PRESS
.COM

Copyright © 2016 by Steve Gilliland

All rights reserved. No part of this book may be used or reproduced in any manner whatsoever without prior written consent of the author, except as provided by the United States of America copyright law.

Published by Pearhouse Press, Pittsburgh, Pennsylvania
pearhousepress.com

Printed in the United States of America.

ISBN: 978-0-9886721-5-4
LCCN: 2016949791

This publication is designed to provide accurate and authoritative information in regard to the subject matter covered. It is sold with the understanding that the publisher is not engaged in rendering legal, accounting, or other professional services. If legal advice or other expert assistance is required, the services of a competent professional person should be sought.

This book is dedicated to the people who hold on to past hurts and often relive the pain over and over again in their minds and get stuck in this pain, in this hurt.

You can't start the next chapter of your life if you are re-reading the last one.

TABLE OF
CONTENTS

The Power to Move Forward

by Bill Wooditch

Founder of Think Next, Act Now!
Bestselling Author of *Always Forward!*

billwooditch.com
allthingsspeaking.com

F lying cross-country offers a respite from the rush to deadline that is life in the achiever's fast lane. The hours can be spent in reflection or study—

"twin-turbo" in the quest to move forward. I was promoting my book *Always Forward!* through different mediums (television, radio, print) in search of a stage where I could live my dream to become a professional speaker. I was searching for a good read—part of that intellectual contract one who continues on the quest for learning makes daily. In my travels, I was made aware of a Hall of Fame Speaker and author of books outlining and offering philosophical and practical ways forward in life. Steve Gilliland was the name that was impressed upon my mind. I had never met Steve, but on a flight to the East Coast I downloaded his book *Making a Difference* on my Kindle. I thought, "This sounds like another book in a long line of rhetoric promising the magic formula to create a difference in life." Most books underserve the potential of these three words by falling short of the means and methods that would provide for their effective application.

From the opening pages, I was surprised and pleased to find something vastly different. Steve's book wasn't rah-rah rhetoric; it was real-life, hard-won experience imbued with a care for others that really did make this book different. I read the entire book, at first looking for the weaknesses or deficiencies in the platform, and then enjoying the ride, embracing the prose and appreciating the style and substance that gave credence to its title. In short, before I had the pleasure of his acquaintance, I became an ardent fan of this man's work.

Some of us may validate through shadows of the past. We have people in our lives we need to please; we seek their attention, applause, respect and approval. There may be something or someone in the past, or perhaps in the present, that provokes this need to validate. Maybe you're told you aren't good enough and you choose to wear that invisible yoke as your reality. It can become a self-fulfilling prophecy that proclaims, "You know what? I'm just not good enough." If you think it long enough, you begin to hobble forward from the crutch of its assumed reality. The hobble grows more pronounced as the yoke of insecurity grows heavier. *Turn the Page* embraces, as fact, the belief that progress will be directly proportional to our ability to effectively engage in the business of life. Business is a subset of life; there are no exclusive domains that house business and life as separate concepts of reality. Every day, I watch people reflect the weariness of past failure on their face. Their body language assumes a posture that signifies

"I am not worthy." We each have a choice—when you become aware that you have the gift of opportunity to change the narrative of your personal story, you can turn the page and make those choices that will liberate and invigorate you. But first, you must find the "book of the self." Take the time and the pain to know yourself, then "Turn the Page" from the power of forward thinking to take those actions that bring meaning to life. The meaning of life is to live it—by moving forward, accepting what cannot be changed and attracting the allies and advocates who can help you make those changes necessary for personal improvement. Choose life over existence!

In *Turn the Page*, you will find that choice takes strength—nothing that is worthy of the effort is easy. But do know this: If you stay in the shadows of those limits long enough, it will become your indelible self-fulfilling prophecy. You will find implicit in the message of *Turn the Page* the question that only you can answer: "Will you allow self-imposed limitations to kill your potential to create a future that is less than what could have been?"

Life is the progeny of the power of forward thinking. The forward-thinking individual asks, "Am I in charge of my own life?" When you adopt this mind-set, you can answer the question consciously. You can make a choice, summon your strength of resolve and do those things that will make a difference by driving you from the rut of the rote toward that which makes you come alive. Growth comes from the new—the new comes from within. It is the byproduct of your personal challenge to learn, adapt, adopt and flourish. But first, you must first turn the page—what you think in the present, what you do from those thoughts, will influence your future. If you stay fixated in the past, you can never grow beyond the limits of its invisible prison. You give up the only thing you have in life: The moment, the "right now"—all else is a dream or a nightmare, a happy thought, a self-inflicted wound or the flags of glory's past that drape you in the faded memories of previous achievements. Life is to live now. The power of forward thinking marries the gift of anticipation to the spirit of action.

Heart and mind generate the pulse and commitment to summon the conviction and the fire to say, "No, I am good enough!" I will prove it to myself by making the choice to change my thoughts and take those actions that are consistent with these thoughts. I will assume the risk and work for the reward. I will turn the page. I will find the power to move forward. I will not accept the surrender to the shadows of past conditions. The voices of the past will not defeat me. They are nothing but the echoes of chosen narrative, constructed memory and fabricated feelings associated with the story I tell myself. I will choose to make the story work for me. I will use past condition or failure as an emotional fuel that will propel my first decisive step forward into a new dawn, a new stage, a new era. I will not crumble and buckle under the belief system of others. I will divest myself of the labels and limitations that emanate from the jealousy, pettiness, weakness or opinion of others. I will work to become aware. I will make the choice and do the work to break through the invisible barriers of limitations. I will accept, forgive or forget those people who, by intent or lack of awareness, attempt to contain or douse my fire of possibility. I will not permit this to happen; I will not wear the opinions of others as fact; I will choose to make my way *mine*.

"It seems that the necessary thing to do is not to fear mistakes, to plunge in, to do the best that one can, hoping to learn enough from blunders to correct them eventually."
— *Abraham Maslow*

Steve encourages the reader to live their best life. He will not dupe the audience. He is intellectually honest in his approach and direct in his delivery. His life experience is forged on the anvil of adversity. He has traveled on the rocky path, removing the barriers to realized possibility each step of the way. He made his way forward in spite of conditions that would discourage and disable many. You have to be willing to pay the price to create the condition— your condition, your lifestyle, your reward, earned from taking the risk, feeling the pain and enjoying the gain that comes from the attempt. *Turn the Page* will provide the way and become the guide in your determination to become a better you today than you were yesterday. Steve is a philosopher at heart and a pragmatist by nature. He knows success is found in the action that propels the way forward one day at a time, one step at a time, one conversation at a time. He knows you don't get to "great"—you don't even pass "good," and you won't collect your $200—by listening to other people who tell you what you can't do. You'll pay a price. The price will include frustration, and the cost will be compounded by failure. But, failure isn't often fatal, and success isn't often final. It's just part of the life process.

Everything of merit is process; everything of gain is *forward*. Nature is aligned with forward motion. Steve didn't make up the rules of life—he just wants for each of you to live your life within the dictates of your nature. The power of forward thinking compels you to face your fears, see them for what they are and watch how the shadows they cast become more insignificant with each bold step you take forward. Accept the acute pain over the chronic dissatisfaction. Accept, address, turn the page, change where you can and accept the consequences of choice. Awareness can offer perspective and appreciation—there is a shortness to this life regardless of span of years. What we focus on becomes our reality. Choose to focus on your internal growth. Understand the purpose of the exercise is to live your best possible life every day, in each connection you forge and in every difference you seek and then make in the life of another.

When we fail to turn the page, when we lose the resolve that resides in the power of forward motion, we sacrifice our self-respect to those in our past—the ghosts, the larger than life issues, the pronounced voices of the naysayers—we renounce the right to our best life.

Steve and I both believe that the magic is all in our minds—that people are just people, we all end up the same way, so let's enjoy the ride. It will determine the nature and quality of the destination. So, while we're here creating and enjoying life, remember, self-respect is dignity personified, integrity lived and character on display. Choose not to give any of it away!

I have had the pleasure of becoming more than a mere acquaintance of Steve's. I consider him a valued friend and mentor. His heart is as vast as his home—an impressive compound where one can create, reset and then move forward to make a difference in the lives of others. While spending time with Steve at his home, we both shared the following thought about writing, teaching and attempting to contribute to the welfare of the whole:

Writers fear leaving the better book in their heads. Will your best possible life fill the pages of the book you author every day? Find the courage to *Turn the Page* and move forward.

Don't fear to begin, but rather fear the future regret of failing to embark.

Steve is giving you your wake-up call. It is both your gift and responsibility to live your life now so one day you can look back and have less regret than you would if you failed to find the power of positive thinking to move forward.

Always Forward!
William S. Wooditch

▶

INTRODUCTION

Dare to Dream Again

Forgiveness requires us to surrender our right to get even. When we forgive, we place the outcome of the matter in God's hands and choose to live with unbalanced scales. It is in accepting this where you will find peace.

I t was my wedding day, a perfect day for an outside ceremony at our country club, and I was marrying my soul mate. I was thirty-six at the time and, ever the good Christian girl, remaining celibate until my vows. He was the answer to my prayers and even better than I had dreamed. I hoped to be as truly happy as my parents, who have been married for over forty years. I felt like Cinderella finally finding her prince and being whisked away into eternal bliss. I now had it all: my own successful company, a man that truly loved me, and I was thin. All that would make this vision complete would be a baby.

I got pregnant almost immediately, another gift from God, as I had struggled with endometriosis, PCOS (polycystic ovarian syndrome) and Hashimoto's thyroiditis. Getting pregnant was only going to happen if God wanted it to. When it did, I could not have been more ecstatic.

On July 25, 2014, my happy ending turned into my worst nightmare. My perfect husband had maxed our joint credit cards. I had excellent credit, you see, and my husband, well, he said his first wife took everything when he divorced her, thus causing his rating to suffer. But how did he spend over $100,000 in less than three months of our marriage? I told him I wanted us to get financial help, and his cryptic response was that he wanted us to keep our finances separate.

That's when, by accident, I found out that my husband—the man of my dreams, my soul mate—

was a bigamist. An IRS bill landed at our house with his ex-wife's name on it. Curious, I called her. "We just got divorced, and he took me for everything!" she said. While sharing all of this with my pastor, I happened to open a medical bill that showed that my husband had been treated for two STDs thirty days after our wedding. When I confronted him about it, he threatened to kill me and said, "I'm done with you!" Then he left me.

In shock, I began to sift through his things over the next few days and found, under our bed, tax returns showing that I was actually his third, possibly fourth, wife. The lies all started to unravel.

My husband's best man—who claimed to be a real estate agent but was really a male stripper— threatened to kill me. He was dumb enough to leave that message on my voicemail, so I had ammunition to obtain a warrant. I broke down in tears as I gave the officer my information, and he kindly called to check on me from time to time, offering me some measure of safety and reassurance.

I had gotten my husband a construction job through business connections and after he left me, I learned that he had been fired. During the first eight months on the job, while we were still together, he would be out in Colorado and would fly back every other week. Only he never came home. His boss told me that he had women regularly visiting his Colorado apartment. It turns out my perfect, born-again Christian husband was a male stripper, just like his best man. He even had a profile on sandiegostrippers.com.

Let's move on…

He told me a friend was taking over the lease of his car, so I mailed back his key. In actuality, however, he abandoned the car on his other wife's front lawn. Her mother, who was on disability, had co-signed for that car and thus became responsible for it. This was one of five cars that my husband had abandoned after having other women co-sign for them. I subsequently learned that many of the charges he put on my credit were work expenses that the company reimbursed him for but for which he pocketed the money.

I was in denial for about a year, embarrassed by what he had done. I was bearing the burden of his indiscretions, but, you see, I was also going to bear his child. I found out I was pregnant about two weeks prior to all of this. Now, nearly two years later, I am still paying off his debts. Yes, I'm responsible for all of it since the credit cards were in my name, even though he committed fraud. He got away with everything. It wasn't until I got a statement from one of his bank accounts that I think all of this cemented in. The last weekend in June 2014, just before I found out about the credit cards, he asked me to extend the limit on the American Express card because he was going to his friend's bachelor party in Vegas. Now, this card was not even open a month and had a $10,000 limit. I said that I couldn't get it higher as I was in shock that he maxed out $10K. He complained that he wouldn't have any money to spend in Vegas. When I got his bank statement in August, though, it showed over $10,000 available, and I saw where he spent $1,000 in Vegas. He was just trying to use me for everything.

So here I was—pregnant, alone and very broke. To make matters worse, he was fired from his job, and that meant bye-bye health insurance. His company said that they would keep me on for a while, but ended up cutting me off without even telling me. The bills were pouring in. The wedding at the country club, the wedding that my parents and I paid for, the tickets we purchased so his family could fly in from Europe, the dream wedding dress, the diamonds that he borrowed money from my parents….My beautiful whole world was shattered because of his lies.

The money he stole kept adding up and up and up. He conned his way out of paying for anything, and me, being the trusting wife, thought everything he told me was the truth. It turned out that he had seventeen liens against him, filed for bankruptcy twice and didn't pay child support for his daughter from a previous marriage. How could this have been the man I married? My dream man?

It would be great if that were the end of the story, but, just like Cinderella, she had a host of bad things happen to her before her real "happy ending."

Remember that really nice police officer who had called to check up on me? He started helping me sort out the legal issues. My husband had committed a felony, bigamy and perjury, along with a multitude of other crimes. To get these prosecuted, I had to work with attorneys I thought might be on my side. Three of them over-billed me by thousands of dollars. These attorneys would not present my case to the District Attorney because apparently, the DA wouldn't prosecute bigamy cases because they were crimes of morality. Had I lived two miles away, across the state border, my husband would have been put away for seven years.

I appealed to the attorney general. Surely, a man who steals over $100,000 from me is worth running in. Nope. The attorney general didn't want to get involved. Why? Politics, it seems. A city council friend of mine said that the governor would prosecute this crime only if I went public to help him against the attorney general, who would be running against him in the next election. So, I'd have to play politics to get this clear-cut crime committed against me prosecuted. Seriously? Can't anyone just do their job?

The state did validate the bigamy by granting me a civil annulment, but the justice system still wouldn't prosecute the crime. They wouldn't even validate that it happened, so my dream-husband-turned-con-man runs free to commit more crimes with no accountability. Since I am an accountability coach, this filled me with anger at our elected officials for not protecting my baby and me.

Well, after running up $50,000 in attorney fees with no results and with all of my husband's debt, I just couldn't afford to pursue the matter any further.

My bigamy attorney then called to suggest we put down on paper that my unborn son was illegitimate. "What?!" I said. "Of course, he's legitimate." "Yes," she said, "but if you say your son is legitimate, then your ex has rights to this baby—and don't be surprised if, given his track record, he tries to use the baby against you for more money."

So now, today, according to the state, I've never been married, had a baby out of wedlock, and my (fake) husband simply abandoned me and his son.

What has happened to me goes beyond a Lifetime movie and feels more like something from *The Twilight Zone*. I came from a good upper middle-class home. I don't (knowingly) hang around with criminals or strippers, so I kept wondering how something so evil could happen to me. "Why me, God? Why didn't You protect me?" Sadly, unlike Cinderella, I was not able to remain courageous and kind. I was not able to forgive and walk away. I'd had it. I let the anger seep into my bones; all I wanted was revenge! Like an abandoned ship taking on gushing seawater, I allowed my circumstance to wholly consume me.

That nice police officer who was comforting me started to come over more often to help me around the house. Before I knew it, my second chance happened. Yes, we fell in love! What an amazing happy ending, right? A police officer rescues a damsel in distress from an evil ex-husband and a coven of wicked attorneys.

But let's just toss another log into the fire, shall we? After nearly a year together, I caught my policeman boyfriend in a few lies—little ones, but hey, by then it didn't take much to make me suspicious, right? I conducted a background check on him. It turns out he was married the whole time. When I confronted him, he said he was emotionally and legally divorced when we met but had stayed married strictly for financial reasons.

When I found his wife's Facebook page and saw them gazing lovingly into each other's eyes, he said that she was in denial about the divorce just like I was too embarrassed to tell people that I was divorced and had been duped by a conniving Lothario. He had a reason for everything. I called his wife. She had no idea about any of this. She said everything was fine and that her husband had mentioned me as being some mental case he met at the airport and that I came on to him. As proof of my sanity and her husband's lies to both of us, I sent her all of the text messages he and I had shared throughout our courtship. *Voila!*

Well, I'd like to say that a (true) prince on a (pure) white horse has shown up on my doorstep and rescued me from all of these horrible men, but I don't have that happy ending, yet. I have never given up hope, however, or lost my resolve. I never want to let any of the bad destroy my optimism or crush my dreams. Am I wary? More than ever!

Whatever your own hellish tale is, fight through the pain. Our lives aren't dictated by what happens to us, but by how we empower ourselves to make better choices and move on. We must be courageous and kind to ourselves and not let the past dictate who we want to become in the future.

There can be an end to pain. You can work through it by *turning the page,* making the pain only a memory rather than a persistent burning ember inside your core. Move on. Persevere. Remember, anyone who is trying to bring you down is already below you. Make your life about rising above. The only way to break the cycle is to be who you really are, which includes the strength, courage and conviction to forgive and let go.

My story isn't fully written yet, and the pages I've shared with you—despite the horrors revealed—will never wipe the smile from my face or shatter the lens of beauty through which I see the world. In the pages to come, you will learn, as Steve Gilliland and his powerful message have so blessedly taught me, to empower yourself by shedding your anger and turning the page. Only then can you see yourself and your world with a better perspective. Only then can you dare to dream again.

▶

1

THE SHAME
OF IT ALL

*Never let your emotions
overpower your intelligence.*

"You listen to me. We all have a destiny, nothing just happens. It's all part of the plan! I should have died out there with my men, but now I am nothing but a cripple. A legless freak! Do you know what it's like not being able to use your legs? Did you hear what I said? You cheated me! I had a destiny. I was supposed to die in the field with honor. That was my destiny and you cheated me out of it. Do you understand what I am saying, Gump? This wasn't supposed to happen. Not to me. I had a destiny. I was Lieutenant Dan Taylor. Look at me. What am I going to do now?"

HIJACKED EXPECTATIONS

In the movie *Forrest Gump*, Lt. Dan went from being a war hero, in his mind, to a legless freak. In an instant, his entire world changed. He went from honor to shame, from significance to worthlessness and from hero to freak. He felt his life was headed somewhere special, but it fell short of his expectations. He hated his new reality. Just like my friend in this book's Introduction who said she felt like Cinderella finally finding her prince and being whisked away into eternal bliss, only to have her enchanted fairytale turned into her worst nightmare. She, too, felt cheated because her destiny and plan were supposed to be different. In her mind, there was no in-between. Either she was going to be blissfully happy or painfully miserable.

Life is full of expectations—those that you develop for yourself, and those that others create for you. These are what you feel you should do, even must do, to fulfill your purpose in life and keep everyone happy. People expect you to be responsible, a loyal friend and family member, a valuable employee—well, you get the idea. Moreover, you expect yourself to be all of these things as well as attractive, engaging, physically fit and financially independent. Your list of expectations is unlimited, but, unfortunately, our reality doesn't always live up to our expectations. As happened with Lt. Dan, my friend's expectations were completely the opposite of her reality. In her mind, she fell short, which, in the end, caused her to blame others, lose hope and even lose her identity.

If you are a moderately adjusted person, falling short of life's expectations may not affect you very much at all. You don't personalize failure as an indictment on your existence. Either you lower your expectations, decide to work a little harder to achieve your expectations or learn to accept your new reality. But, Steve, aren't we supposed to always raise our expectations to new summits? You know, shoot for the moon and you'll land in the stars. Until you are able to fall short of your life's expectations without it having a devastating outcome, then the answer is no.

When we personalize our failure as a statement of our worth, we allow it to define us.

Somewhere in our past, we were taught that performance determines your worth, and if we aren't exceeding expectations, we aren't valuable. That, my friend, is shame!

REJECTION IS REDIRECTION

I remember the first time I went furniture shopping with my wife, Diane. We no sooner walked into Havertys furniture store in Winston-Salem, North Carolina when she said, "We need to go upstairs to the second floor in the back where they keep the damaged goods. If it's not perfect, they won't display it. They don't believe it has much value so they will mark it down." Much to my astonishment, the furniture was striking in spite of a few chips and marks.

Maybe that's how you feel? Good for nothing. Maybe you've been divorced, not once but twice, or even more. Perhaps you have lost your job, or you just seem to keep attracting the wrong people. In your mind, these chips and scratches have made you question your value. You have convinced yourself that something must be wrong with you, so you go through life anticipating rejection at every turn.

Rejection is merely redirection. My friend is bitter and angry; however, I am confident she is going to come to appreciate more than she could ever imagine because of her situation.

Rejection is not someone wanting her out of his life. Rejection is someone that God wanted out of her future.

The key to dealing with anger isn't so much whether you get angry or not, but in how long you allow the anger to remain with you and how you process your emotion. The pain of shame looks for someone to blame. It causes you to blame yourself for failing to reach your expectations, blame others for criticizing or rejecting you, and blame the other person for decisions you willingly made. Blame feeds anger.

EVENING THE SCORE

On the other hand, if you direct your anger toward your wrongdoer, you can't forgive and still be angry. Being angry with your offender is a form of retaliation—the opposite of forgiveness. People feel the need to even the score and can't rest until they do. This is what gets us into trouble, causing us to waste years and energy getting back at someone, even if it's just us wishing them harm in our minds.

If you've given up the right to get even with your offender, that's forgiveness; however, if your loss still hurts, that's a normal emotion that will exist as long as you feel the loss. As you come to accept the loss and move on with your life, the anger and shame will slowly dissipate.

Until you turn the page, you will still harbor anger even though you have chosen not to get back at your offender. The feeling comes from not being able to control your loss. Being powerless makes you mad, but you can still forgive.

PAIN PRODUCES MOVEMENT

While people respond to the pain and shame of wrong choices in a variety of ways, there are three actions that are consistent with most DNA: we either move toward people, against them or away from them.

If confession truly is good for the soul, then here goes. Because of my hurting past, I move *toward* others with people pleasing and caretaking behavior so they will like me. I sharpen my perfectionist skills to make sure I never upset anyone, so the compliments continue my way. Every encounter is an opportunity to prove my worth.

Others move *against* people with anger. Their wounds keep them on high alert to the slightest invalidation, causing them to strike out in retaliation.

Unfortunately, their aggressive behavior may not be just an offensive tactic punishing people for hurting them; it could be a defensive tactic designed to keep them at arm's length.

> **We train people with our anger to walk on eggshells around us so they won't get too close and expose our flaws.**

Likewise, there are those who choose to move *away* and shut down emotionally, withdrawing physically and taking great strides to cover up any pain or shame. Their objective is to disconnect from anyone they perceive to be a threat, creating the distance necessary to limit the exposure of their weakness.

Sadly, none of these reactions do anything to unscramble the pain and, in some instances, they even establish more pain. Let's be clear about one thing, though. I've learned that most people don't want to talk about their pain or shame. It hurts too much or is embarrassing to admit to. They would rather forget.

In the moment of pain, they are coping the best they can with the knowledge they have.

LET GO OF YOUR NONSENSE

Being the victim feels good. It's like being on the winning team of you against the world. Regrettably, the world doesn't care, so you need to get over yourself. Don't misinterpret what I am saying. You are special and your feelings matter; however, don't allow your feelings to override all else to the mistake of nothing else matters. Your feelings are just one part of this vast thing we call life, which is all interwoven and complex. And some days a little bit messy!

In every moment you have a choice. You can continue to feel bad about another person's actions—or start feeling good. You need to take responsibility for your own happiness and not put so much power into the hands of another person.

Why would you let the person who hurt you, in the past, have so much power, right here and right now?

No amount of contemplation, analysis or evaluation has ever fixed a relationship problem. Never! So why choose to engage so much thought and devote so much energy to a person you feel has wronged you?

PAIN CONTROL

What you've done, or what's been done to you, is not the power of pain. The power of pain is what you believe! You live what you believe. If you believe your house is haunted, your house is haunted. If you believe you are worthless, you won't treat yourself well emotionally, physically or spiritually because you are convinced you aren't worth it. Healing the hurts of your past involves eliminating the lies from your life. Pain has little to do with the bad things that have happened to you or the bad things you have done. Pain has everything to do with the lies you believe about yourself. Lt. Dan believed he was only appreciated as a war hero and that his value was based on his performance. That, my friend, is the shame of it all.

▶

2

LIFE IS A DO-IT-YOURSELF PROJECT

It takes forever to find yourself, but it only takes one second to forget who you are.

W hether you've lost yourself in your career as a result of a bad relationship or simply feel lost, in general, trust me when I say, you are not alone. It doesn't mean you are destined to be satisfied with "settling." It just means you are going through a maturation period.

MAKE PEACE WITH YOURSELF

As you begin new chapters in your life, ask yourself some questions: *What are my goals and objectives? What is my plan to achieve those? What skills do I need to acquire or modify to better equip myself to meet my expectations?* While I cannot tell you precisely how to answer these questions, I can share what worked best for me. Too many people try to turn the page without letting go of the regrets from previous chapters in their lives. Regret is a tough feeling to shake. It preoccupies you in ways that will demoralize you and inhibit your ability to let go of the past and improve your future. Anytime you look back you can recall several things you wish you had done differently. The key is to keep those things in perspective and accept them as an inevitable part of growth.

I had many misgivings about several aspects of my life, especially the role I played with my sons during their adolescent years; however, it doesn't help much to dwell on what I did or didn't do. At the time, I did the very best I could, given my knowledge and experience. I did not do anything deliberately to let my sons down even though I might have wrongly applied some of my good intentions. Now, having two stepsons, I have come to terms with my past mistakes and accepted them as pointers from which I have discovered some helpful lessons. You can learn from past mistakes, but you can't undo them. Dwelling on them and becoming obsessed by them will unavoidably affect your family, friends, career and every other aspect of your life.

TAKE INVENTORY

Do you remember when Don Meredith was part of the broadcast team for *Monday Night Football*? Besides dating yourself as I just did, you will smile at the remembrance of the lyrics he would sing late in a game, "Turn out the lights, the party's over..." With those words, "Dandy" Don was indicating to viewers that the game was so far out of reach that it might as well end even though there was still time left on the clock. The certainty of any circumstance can disclose a fact that will not permit you to believe it wholly, which ultimately directs you to repeat the same mistakes.

We have an intrinsic sense that if we do the same thing on a different day the result may change. We read the same page of our life hoping it has changed since the last time we examined it. When you conclude that "the party's over," it's time for you to be honest with yourself. Face the tough questions and realize where you are, how you got there and whom you have impacted along the way.

Being willing to ask the tough question isn't the hard part. It is having the guts to answer the question honestly.

It is about ascertaining who you are or, as some counselors suggest, taking the time to discover yourself. For almost forty years of my life, I, in fact, believed I needed to be someone else. In an attempt to climb the ladder professionally and socially, I never exposed the real me. My goal was always to be what I perceived other people wanted me to be and, moreover, what I perceived true success to be. For me, it was all about being liked and having people accept as true something that wasn't. Even when I struggled financially, I continued to pick up the tab at restaurants just to impress the people I was with. Furthermore, I was suppressing who I truly was to please my mother and my in-laws. As strict Christians, they shared strong opinions regarding any lifestyle that didn't fit their religious views. Not that their views were wrong, but they were theirs, not necessarily mine.

As a substitute for taking stock of who I was and living that life, I determined it was easier to let my bold nature turn into questionable choices, which would eventually lead me down painful paths. I unwisely set aside some things that were important to me, which would prove to be unsettling in my life. When I, at last, hit the wall, everything that meant anything to me had vanished. Only then did I do some soul searching and answer the tough questions

I needed to ask myself. I longed to have power over my state of affairs, but I just didn't know how to go about it.

SEIZE CONTROL OF YOUR EGO

How we think and how we respond have a far greater capacity to tear down our lives than any challenge we face. How quickly we respond to misfortune is far more important than adversity itself. The greatest challenge of life is to be in command of the process of our own thinking. We all have experienced distress, misery and heartbreak, but why do people arrive at such diverse places at the end of the journey? Ego! It gets in the way and seats us in our current circumstances. Not until we begin to live a life based on who we are, in fact, will we ever truly accomplish what we are capable of.

If you want to turn the page, you have to merge your ego with the aspiration of your soul.

In spite of our best efforts, we have moments when things just seem to fall apart. It is during these times that you must be true to who you are and allow your soul—not your ego—to steer you. To help you distinguish between your ego and your soul, and assist you in comprehending why they can be counterproductive if not fused within your inner self, here are six contrasts.

EGO	SOUL
Reactive	Creative
Driven by fear	Centered in peace
Lives in the past	Lives in destiny
About surviving	About the journey (*Enjoy The Ride!*)
Focuses on what's wrong	Looks for meaning
Low trust in others	Faith in others

If there was ever an epiphany in my life, it was when I discovered that my ego was in command of my soul. Discovering the real Steve was not just a turning point that would shape my life, it would become an intricate part of my personal and professional beliefs today. When I realized who I was and, more importantly, who I most wanted to be, my life changed dramatically. Then and only then was I truly capable of mastering myself and turning the page.

> **The greatest challenge in life is discovering who you are. The second greatest challenge in life is being happy with what you find.**

Counselors implore people to discover themselves. In doing so, they ask what it is that makes life worthwhile for us? They also want us to outline where we want to go and what we are yearning to see. The discovery process includes questions about our career, where we aspire to live and dreams we may have. *Where do you see yourself five years from now? Who will be a part of your life and play a significant role in it five years from now? Are the people who are currently in your inner circle of friends helping you or hurting you?* All great questions that, when answered, will help you better know yourself. However, the number one question that needs to be answered first is, "Who are you?"

More importantly, who do you want to be? How much disparity is there between who you are and the person your family, friends and colleagues see you as? The time is now for you to unite your ego with the ambition of your soul and begin the evolutional improvement toward becoming your true self. When you admire people for a set of values you want, but don't possess, commit yourself to being that person and being the difference maker you were intended to be.

CREATE YOURSELF

To remember who you are, forget what they told you to be. Everything you think you need to be successful is in your life already. You chase money, fame, material possessions and experiences that never fill you up completely. Your focus shifts to being the person your ego drives you to believe people will be more receptive to. Ironically, you begin to attract who you are (or, in this case, are not), and when the real you emerges, there is a colossal variance between the true you and the people you have attracted. All too often the hidden you is never allowed to surface, and you live a segment of your life playing a character frantically trying to be accepted.

When your ego interrupts who you really are, you tend to chase after things outside of yourself to find fulfillment.

From grade school through high school, all I wanted was to be accepted as one of the cool kids in school. I did everything, and anything to be that guy, but regrettably was never true to myself. As a young adult, I alternated between my ego and my soul. The generous, caring, loyal person I am was too often overrun by my self-centeredness and insensitivity. Those who knew me well could only wonder why my actions didn't match my beliefs. The good news is that regardless of who we pretend to be, the real us is still sheathed within and when released, allows us to rediscover so many things that were already a part of us. The Steve Gilliland that family, friends and acquaintances had come to know would elicit doubts as to whether or not they thought I was capable of changing—of turning the page. More often than I care to remember, all I heard was, "We'll see." While it didn't take place overnight, I am pleased to have discovered that life isn't about finding yourself. Life is about creating yourself. The funny thing is, the more I find myself, the more people I lose along the way.

▶

3

STOP CHASING TWO RABBITS

Change your priorities and
you change your life.

No activity will impact your ability to turn the page and influence the direction and progress of your life more than setting priorities. You can have all the determination, discipline, motivation and inspiration that you want, but if your efforts are scattered or misdirected, you will have little impact. If you chase two rabbits, you will never catch either one of them.

KEEP THE FAITH

In my darkest hour, with my theological and doctrinal formulations in question, I never doubted God. I remember thinking that my circumstances weren't something I could dispel by waving a magic wand or dream my way out of, but rather something that only trust could rescue me from. I remember saying a prayer that, in retrospect, was probably the beginning of when I started to turn the page. I asked God to forgive me for my choices and help me to make better ones. I prayed that my marriage could recover and solicited Him to give me a second chance. God would give me a second chance; however, it wasn't exactly what I had prayed for. God's blueprint for me was already written. I guess when Garth Brooks wrote the song "Unanswered Prayers," he had me in mind. The assurance I had was that my prayers were answered in accordance to His will, not mine. I look back from where I am today and marvel at how everything unfolded. It is amazing what happens when you keep the faith and rely solely on God.

DON'T WASTE SECOND CHANCES

Life always offers second chances. It's called tomorrow. Chuck Gallagher is a dear friend of mine who is an incredible speaker and the author of a book entitled *Second Chances*. In the book, Chuck comes clean about his past, his mistakes and what they taught him as he rebuilt his life. Although he enjoyed a good life and a steady job, greed got the better of him and, little by little, he began to steal from his clients. It was only a matter of time before his choices caught up to him. After his stunning and public fall from the graces of his community, Chuck describes his life in prison, the things he missed out on and the steps he took to make things right. His inspiring story focuses on how we can transform our worst moments into better opportunities. When you hear him tell his story, you begin to realize what J.K. Rowling meant when she said, "Rock bottom became the solid foundation on which I rebuilt my life." Chuck is quick to point out that everybody deserves a second chance—but not for the same mistake. When you finally stop trying to even the score with someone, you will recognize that what you have endured allows you to initiate a new course. Don't be afraid to start over. It's another chance to rebuild.

WHAT REALLY MATTERS

The key to second chances and pursuing new opportunities is to get your life's priorities in order. Prioritizing your life includes achieving a healthy balance in relationships with families and friends.

You can never make the same mistake twice. The second time it's not a mistake—it's a choice.

There is nothing wrong with starting a new business, but in talking to thousands of entrepreneurs, I have learned that their greatest regret was not the big deal they missed, but the time they lost being with the ones they loved. I speak from experience. My two sons, Stephen and Josh, nieces Crystal and Heidi, and nephew Brock grew up, and I missed too many occasions to share special moments. Time is so very precious.

Pursuing new endeavors is another chance to do right, not repeat the same mistakes. Don't *again* neglect your family or your friends. Don't neglect your health or your spiritual life either. Balance is essential. We rarely succeed at anything unless we have fun doing it.

IT'S NEVER TOO LATE

Let's talk for a minute about a woman named Colette Bourlier. Her remarkable story came across my desk just today. As her name might imply, Colette lives in France. She just earned her Ph.D. in history. That's a pretty tough feat at any age, but Colette is 91! At 91, she had to hobble in front of an academic committee to defend her thesis. As she defended the thesis over the two-hour cross-examination, she had to sit very close to the panel, as she is going deaf. She would not be denied. Indeed, the thesis defense called on her to introduce a large volume of very complex material.

Her professor stated, "She is probably the only person who knew all the aspects in such detail and who was able to weave everything together. She backed it up with statistical analyses."

By the way, she did not start the pursuit of the doctorate until she had *retired* at 61!

Still not impressed? The academicians marked Dr. Bourlier's thesis with the grade of High Distinction and, though this should not surprise anyone, she is the oldest woman in France ever to earn a Ph.D. What fascinates me the most about Colette Bourlier is the fact that the thesis took so long for her to research and write. When questioned about this, she said, succinctly, "It took a bit of time to write because I took breaks." I guess one might conclude that she enjoyed the ride.

Balance is not something you find; it is something you create.

Were those breaks due to family commitments? Did she go on extended vacations? Was she pursuing hobbies? She didn't say, but what is apparent is that she kept her life balance, she continued pursuing her dream, and she refused to quit. Colette kept her priorities in order.

What can *you* be doing right now? If you have ever heard me speak, then you know I am grounded in reality. I understand that you may not be able to change your life in any way you want right now. There are real limits in most people's lives, and personal development isn't magic that can fix just about anything quickly and easily. However, you can do what you can do with what you have where you are right now if you have balance and faith in yourself. As for Dr. Bourlier, I have little doubt that she is thinking about her next project!

ACQUIRE SELECTIVE HEARING

If you are willing to change, everything can, and will, change for you. One of the reasons people don't do well is because they keep trying to get through the day instead of getting something from the day. Pay attention during your day, watch what's going on and become a good listener. Surround yourself with people you respect and admire. My mother has always preached the same sermon when it comes to relationships: "Surround yourself with a character of people that bear a resemblance to who you want to become." Find people whose personalities and achievements stimulate, fascinate and inspire you and then strive to duplicate their patterns of superiority. Or, as Mark Victor Hansen has stated from the platform, "Duplicate patterns of excellence." Monitor and think about what is happening around you.

Often, the most extraordinary opportunities are hidden among insignificant events.

As you listen, be selective. With so many opinions and voices vying for your attention, you have to be discerning and fortify your listening proficiency. If a voice is not leading to the achievement of your goals, exercise caution in how long you listen.

As a member of the National Speakers Association, I regularly caution new speakers to be judicious in accepting all the direction they hear from their contemporaries. There is an abundance of ideas, volumes of best practices and countless beliefs about how to build a successful speaking business. Nonetheless, what works for one speaker may not work for the rest. The key is to be aligned with people who are moving in the precise direction you want to go. It is one thing to announce you are heading to Pennsylvania; it is an entirely different thing to say whether you want to end up in Pittsburgh or Philadelphia. As you turn the page, be sure to head in the right direction.

BE DISCIPLINED

Every day is filled with dozens of personal crossroads, moments when you're called upon to make decisions regarding minor as well as major questions. These decisions chart a path to a future destination and ultimately determine your happiness and success. With vigilant intellectual preparation, you can make prudent choices. It is essential that you make fitting decisions. Anytime I eat right and exercise, I experience positive results and feel vitality almost immediately. The key—discipline! The same can be said of reading. At a conference I once attended, Zig Ziglar challenged the audience to read more and become a carnivore of information. When you begin reading, you experience a growing awareness and new levels of self-confidence. Granted, some things you already know are said in a different way, but the question is whether or not it affirms what you are doing or reminds you of what you are not doing. New disciplines practiced daily will produce exciting results. Turning the page requires new disciplines that will cause us to amend our thinking and change our priorities.

▶

4

STOP WATERING DEAD PLANTS

It is better to be alone than in bad company.

F riendship has taken on a different meaning these days. For example, we have "Friends" on Facebook, many of whom we hardly know! We have friends at work, who are usually people we're *friendly with* during the eight or so hours we're together, and then some friends live in our neighborhood. We wave to them, invite them over for an occasional gathering, share some food and beverages, but know little about them.

The friends I am talking about in this book are those who are really in our lives—those with whom we have shared experiences, personal dreams and wishes and those with whom we have been vulnerable. I am talking about true, not digital or activity-related, friends.

Friendships can fill our hearts and bring us great joy. Friends can give us sustenance and help nurture us, especially through rough patches. Friends can share our life's histories and help us mark important events. It goes almost without saying that many of our friends can often be closer than family. Our friends often become our families.

THE REAL DEAL

When we lose a digital friend, recovery from such a tragedy is usually brief. In fact, for those who link their success in life to their vast numbers of friends or connections or followers, they may not even know they've suffered a loss for months!

The losses of friendships that truly get to our hearts are the three-dimensional sort—real and deeply personal. Such losses can upset us, and we can even be in mourning over them if we allow ourselves to be.

Sometimes the loss of a friendship can be exactly what we need. In fact, losing a friend can be more important than maintaining the "friendship." Am I a callous or insensitive person here? No, not at all. It is time to talk about a painful topic that may, in actuality, be joyous.

A friendship that can end never really began.

Recently, I conducted an informal poll among my friends as to why a previous "good" friendship may have faded, dried up and blown away. As we sat around the fire pit, their informal responses taught me what I already knew: friendships fade for real reasons. In one case, a friend was undermining and demanding. In another, a friend had become too much of a drinking buddy, where alcohol became more important than conversation. Then there was a case where a friend had turned angry and overly opinionated, finding fault with everything and everybody to the point of discomfort. One of those I surveyed expressed that friends who had "perfect" children amazed them. One vented, "I think it's funny that people who treat you offensively get offended when you finally do the same to them." When the exchange had come full circle (literally) around the fire, and it was my turn to share, I simply said that I would rather be known in life as an honest sinner than a lying hypocrite.

Though other aspects of the friendship might have had their better memories and shared experiences, the "tests" we are made to go through as a result of maintaining loyalty are just not worth the effort or the pain. Finally, one day, we realize it is less important to have more friends and more important to have real ones.

EVERY END IS A NEW BEGINNING

At first, when the people I spoke with realized a friendship was over, they were (naturally) sad. Some expressed that such a loss was painful. Then, as the "friendship" slipped away, there was a slow awakening that maybe it was a good thing. Some of their realizations were:

+ *"I am becoming happier. I didn't want to be around all that anger and negativity."*

+ *"I did not want the only thing we had in common to be drinking!"*

+ *"I am not a two-faced person, and I don't want to be around someone who is!"*

+ *"I realized that once fake friends stop talking to you, they start talking about you."*

The realizations were not only healthy; but they were also extremely valid. What would have been disturbing is if they *stayed* in those friendships.

Good friends care for each other, while close friends understand each other. A real friend either apologizes or at least talks about it, but a fake friend talks to their spouse or others about it. Genuine friends stay forever, beyond words, distance and time. Through the years, one of the best lessons I have learned is that being honest may not get you a lot of friends, but it will always get you the right ones.

There are simply times in our lives when we are much happier leaving than staying, when the journey must end for us to move on and have more fulfilling and meaningful relationships. Remember when you were a kid and were happy for no reason? Be that again. The best feeling in the world is when you realize turning the page on a friendship allows you to recognize there is so much more to the book than the page you are stuck on. In life, we never lose friends. We only learn who the true ones are.

LET THEM WALK

The hardest part of turning the page concerns people. People who were a part of your past and, when the challenging times materialized, ostensibly vanished.

People you treated like relatives and considered as friends simply walked out of your life to go a different direction. I would have never predicted that certain people would have walked away from me. The struggle I had was letting them walk. My counselor, Herb, always said, "Don't try to talk your wife into staying with you, loving you, calling you, caring about you, coming to see you, staying attached to you. If she can walk away from you, let her walk. Your destiny will not be tied to anyone who is willing to walk out of your life." The Bible says, "They came out from us that it might be made manifest that they were not for us. For had they been of us, no doubt they would have continued with us." [1 John 2:19]

Not all people in your life are meant to stay.

It doesn't mean they are bad people. It just means that their role in the story is over. The rough part is comprehending when a person's part in your story is over so that you don't keep trying to revive something that should be gone forever. You've got to know when it's over. It took me a long time to acquire the gift of good-bye. I know whatever God means for me to have He'll give me, and if it takes too much fret and worry I usually don't need it. After my ex-wife determined that her life would better without me, it took me several months before I stopped petitioning her to stay and simply let her go.

SEE WHAT YOU BELIEVE

In order to turn the page, if you are holding on to something that doesn't belong to you and was never intended for your life, then you need to let go. If you are holding on to past hurts and pains, let go. If someone can't treat you right, love you back and see your worth, let go. If someone repeatedly has and intentionally angered you, let go. If you are holding on to some thoughts of evil and revenge, let go. If you are involved in a wrong relationship or dependence, let go. If you are holding on to a job that no longer meets your needs or abilities, let go. If you have a dire attitude, let go. If you keep judging others to make yourself feel better, let go. If you are struggling with the healing of a broken relationship, let go. If you keep trying to help someone who won't even try to help themselves, let go. If you're feeling depressed and stressed, let go.

Accept what is, let go of what was and have faith in what will be.

Take responsibility for your past, start a new chapter and let go. You can't change yesterday, but you can ruin today worrying about tomorrow. Instead of reading the same page over and over, turn the page. It's time to start a new chapter and not let history dictate the rest of your life. Ex means thanks for the EXperience. Our time has EXpired. Now EXit my life. I am finished watering dead plants.

YOU ARE STRONGER THAN YOU THINK

At some point, while turning the page, you hopefully will be ready to become what you are intended to be, in conflict will be your old personality still trying to please and impress everyone. Regardless of where you are, who is a part of your life and how unappealing the future may appear, the next pages of your life can be enriching and fulfilling. From time to time, however, we are disinclined to change anything because we enjoy the reassurance of familiarity. The courage to broaden your horizons takes more than a desire to change. It requires motivation and strength to change with the realization that, if you don't, your passage may fall short given your opposition to transforming.

Like it or not, the world evolves, priorities change and so do you.

As I turned the page in my life, I walked down an abandoned path. My friends and family who were a part of my life disappeared for a period of time. My father in no way ever played a meaningful role in my life, and my mother was disappointed in me, whereas my brother was blissfully content with his life, and my circumstances seemed inconsequential. My so-called friends were all gone. Although my faith in people evaporated, the lessons it taught me still serve me today.

I recognized that if you spend too long holding on to the one who treats you like an option, you'll miss finding the one who treats you like a priority. Don't worry about people from your past. There is a reason why they didn't make it to your future. Stop watering things that were never meant to grow in your life.

▶

THE PATH
LESS
TRAVELED

*Only the walls you build
yourself confine you.*

When you forgive and still hold a grudge, it's like driving forward with your foot on the brake. Anyone can hold a grudge, but it takes a person with character to forgive. When you forgive, you release yourself from a painful burden. It doesn't mean what happened was okay, and it doesn't mean that the offending person should still be welcome in your life. It just means you made peace with pain and are ready to let it go.

THE GIFT YOU GIVE YOURSELF

It took me twelve years to visit my father's grave. Writing this book was the impetus. At his gravesite, I asked him many questions and made many statements. I have wondered about so many things throughout the years. I wanted most of all to know why he could never to tell me he loved me. We are all aware that what happens to us in childhood has an effect upon who we become as adults. The accomplishments, mistreatment and even abuse all have an impact. While I was never abused or mistreated, my father never recognized my accomplishments. Moreover, what had the most profound effect on me was the emotional neglect.

A wound gets worse when it's treated with neglect.

Emotional neglect is, in some ways, the opposite of mistreatment and abuse. Whereas mistreatment and abuse are actions, emotional neglect is a failure to act. It's a failure to notice, attend to or respond appropriately to a child's feelings. Because it's an act of omission, it is felt, not witnessed. Emotional neglect is the white space in the family picture, the background rather than the foreground. It is deceptive and often overlooked while it does its silent damage to people's lives.

Because my father never validated my emotions as a child, I grew up having difficulty knowing and trusting my own emotions. Not only did I struggle to understand my own feelings, but I also didn't appreciate other people. An important part of me had been denied, and I sometimes felt disconnected, unfulfilled and empty. I have always struggled to trust and to rely upon others. For too many years I blamed myself. Then, it became fitting to blame my father. Today, I have released the pain by offering forgiveness and realizing I don't need to know the answers to any questions. I didn't forgive my father because I am weak; I forgave him because I have become strong enough to know people make mistakes.

FORGIVING IS NOT FORGETTING

You must let go of pain and resentment before the healing power of forgiveness can occur. However, in addition to resentment, you also need to let go of your misconceptions about forgiveness. Forgiving is not forgetting. Nor is it exempting someone from the responsibility for what they have done. Forgiving does not have the power to ease all of your hurt feelings. The power of forgiveness does not involve magically returning relationships to the state they were in before hurt took place. Forgiveness is the canceling of a debt and the beginning of the healing process. Forgiveness takes practice.

BE A LIMITED EDITION

Every day, there are signs, messages and guideposts that will inspire you to act, but you only notice them if you are quiet and listening. With all the noise, mindless chatter and need to be "connected," it can be difficult to recognize the signs that are all around, so it's important to tune in. Pay attention to the signs on the road, songs on the radio and people you meet. People always ask me where I get my material for my stories, books and humor. Life! I observe people and situations that are messengers all around me. More than once, I have found answers to questions on a billboard, in a magazine advertisement or from a single line spoken in a movie. The key is to pay attention.

The simple act of paying attention can take you a long way.

Try getting away from the mental pain and hulla-baloo by taking a trip. Explore the world and focus on actually reconnecting with yourself. You need a fresh perspective, and being away from the noise of your regular life will allow you to see the world with fresh eyes. When I began to turn the page, I did just that. I took a weeklong trip by myself—and found it very uncomfortable trying new things and meeting new people. I soon realized that growth doesn't happen by staying in your comfort zone where everything is familiar. Try stretching yourself to grow and evolve. I strongly encourage you to do whatever comes to mind first. Don't color outside the lines or inside the lines. Just color. Don't think outside the box or inside the box. Get rid of the box all together. When you're in your own lane, there is no traffic.

PAVED WITH GOOD INTENTIONS

I still believe that most people mean well, and when they give us bad advice, it's coming out of their own misconceptions. Most people have no expertise in the complex dynamics of human behavior. Moreover, too many give advice based on their own fears, beliefs and expectations. People who know you tend to have incorrect assumptions about what would make you happy. They think you should make the same choices they would in similar situations. A great example is when individuals seek advice from their pastor. I understand and respect the role of the pastor; however, the advice they give isn't always objective or tailored to our individual needs. It's so easy to believe someone when they're telling you exactly what you want to hear.

> **When you want to help people, you tell them the truth. When you want to help yourself, you tell them what they want to hear.**

Most of the time, people, especially our friends, are trying to help us. They sincerely believe that what they're saying is in our best interests. We need to see that, even though they love us and know us to some extent, they don't always know what's right for us. Some of our friends bring their own emotional baggage to the act of advice giving. Their desperation for love, their willingness to tolerate disrespect and their ability to settle for less strongly affect the relationship advice they give to us. Our friends may be wonderful people, but their advice can sometimes be useless and sometimes even risky. Our close friends identify with us. Without realizing it, they project their own needs, anxieties and insecurities onto us. Despite their wanting the best for us, they'd have us making the same mistakes too. The people who love you want you to be happy. However, people only know what their version of happiness looks like at work and in life.

STOP SCRATCHING THE SCAB

Do you hold grudges? Do you have a hard time letting go of that angry, frustrated feeling that comes when you feel as though somebody's wronged you? Do you still hold on to that little kernel of anger and bitterness and take it out and poke at it when the nights are long and you can't sleep? Do you even have a perverse part of yourself that hopes someone you're upset at hears about how well you are doing, preferably through an unconnected third party for that extra "how do you like me now?" You're not alone! I am willing to bet most, if not all, people carry around a secret resentment.

We all have someone in our lives who hurt us, betrayed us, wronged us; someone we still resent, whose very name curdles our blood and makes us grit our teeth in frustration because they stubbornly refuse to evaporate from the face of the earth. Sometimes it's a friend. Sometimes it's a lover. And why are breakups that may have been equally your fault so hard to let go of, even when there is no reason to hold on? Even in circumstances when you unequivocally have the upper hand and win, you still feel anger.

Sometimes it's not getting your heart ripped out that hurts as much as the pinpricks to your ego.

Sometimes it's the feeling of an unaddressed injustice that spurs us on. Sometimes it's simply the fact that the universe seems to be taking its own sweet time noticing that you've been wronged, and we want karma to finally come back around. However, most times it is because we are looking for a magical moment that will bring us closure.

It's hard to let go of negative emotions under the best of circumstances. These are people who have occupied significant space in our heads and hearts, sometimes for years. We continue to let them rent space in our minds and find it hard to evict them even when they deserve it. Unfortunately, we don't let the wounds heal. We encourage them to irritate and fester by constantly picking at the scabs. Of course, healing is easier said than done. Thanks to a world where we are continuously connected to one another through our mobile devices via social media, it is becoming harder not to reopen wounds. We are able to secretly stick our noses into almost anyone's life and stalk them undetectably on Twitter and Instagram. We even dig through their unsecured Facebook accounts to see what they are up to. We rationalize our behavior by saying that it is all done to help avoid running into them in social situations. Please! Be honest! You're checking on them to see if they are happy. If they are happy, it is the ultimate dose of salt being poured into the open wound. They hurt us, and they need to be punished. They need to suffer!

The hardest part is to accept that it's not fair, and there is nothing you can do about it. Part of why we hold on to this anger with people who've wronged us is because we desperately want validation for not just our pain, but their role in it. There's no guarantee that you will ever get them to admit they have hurt you.

> **Sometimes a person's refusal to confess their guilt and take responsibility is a matter of protecting their own ego.**

We all want to be heroes of our own stories and, ideally, we like to keep that vision intact. Admitting fault means you have to surrender and take the moral high road. Some people are simply oblivious to the fact that they've done anything wrong in the first place. Regardless of whether they're sociopathic or simply self-absorbed, there is no way of actually getting them to see things your way. From their vantage point, there was no wrongdoing, and you're just being dramatic.

CLOSURE IS A MYTH

The need for closure is the need for validation, vindication and for things to line up in the way you feel the world should work. Most times that is not going to happen. Closure doesn't come when you've had one last talk or confrontation. It doesn't come when you've reached some level of success or achieve an amazing lifestyle that they can't help but be jealous of.

Going back and rehashing old conflicts and scratching the scabs off of old wounds in the name of closure is a recipe for misery.

Your obsession with winning or getting power back only gives them greater mindshare in your life. It lets them continue to poison your soul, no matter who was actually in the wrong. All that fixating about your hurt and betrayal does nothing but give the apparition in your mind more power to hurt you. Others can't give closure, and it only comes when you decide you have it. Period.

Learning to let go of past hurt and anger is hard, but it is critical. It is imperative that you cut all ties, including blocking the offending parties on all your social media accounts, deleting their numbers and texts from your phone and erasing their emails and any other form of contact you may have had with them. Eliminating them from your life as much as possible makes it harder to pick at the scab. If you encounter them in a social circle, simply disregard them. To make them an issue is to give them the power to continue to hurt you. To lessen their importance, to make them no more significant than a random face in the crowd, steals their ability to mess with you.

Next, you have to forgive them by forgiving yourself. Blaming ourselves for being part of the drama, for letting ourselves be hurt, is what keeps us from being able to let go. It's only when you can forgive yourself for getting hurt that you can start to heal. The key to getting past any transgression is to understand the role you played and learn how to keep something like that from ever happening again. The value of the lesson learned allows you to feel better about admitting your involvement and knowing in your heart that the mistake will never be repeated.

You may never find yourself in a place where you never think of them again, and that's okay. The point of closure isn't to eliminate them from your memory; it's simply to end the pain, and it's impossible to accomplish that when you let it be part of your present. Accept that you've found your closure and put it in the past where it belongs. The only way to bring closure is to stop building walls. The walls that you believe are keeping people out are merely confining you. This is a path not often traveled, but when it is taken, the outcomes are surprising.

▶

6

IF IT'S NOT OKAY, IT'S NOT THE END

Don't stare at the closed door too long or you'll miss the window opening.

Endurance is the restrained side of perseverance. The Serenity Prayer cautions us to focus our efforts on what we can change and accept what we cannot. "When external circumstances rain on our parade, patience is our umbrella. Instead of blaming what we cannot control, patience gives us pause for reflection so we can dry off and start looking for the sun to come out. Everything over time is either ongoing or off going," says author and speaker Dennis Waitley. You can't undo everything overnight. It took me the better part of a decade to reach the point where I am today and, for what it's worth, it isn't easy.

KEEP HOLDING ON

A clear picture of what you should do with the rest of your life may not surface anytime soon. Even when I took responsibility for my situation, the situation was real and continued to be a part of my life. The bills didn't stop arriving in my mailbox, and I was about to be out of work. To make matters worse, I would be in constant view of the people I once tried to impress, only to have them sneer, deride and mock my failures. When I attended my son's high school sporting events, it was a feeding frenzy for these people.

Focus your efforts on what you can change and accept what you cannot.

My solution was to be determined and endure the new ride regardless of how long it would take and how many obstacles I would have to overcome. There is no step-by-step system that, when followed, guarantees everything will turn out right. The foremost predicament occurs whenever the new blueprint doesn't work quite the way you envisioned, you get disheartened, and you start going backward instead of forward. Prior to meeting my wife Diane, there were some significant barriers regarding my post-divorce relationships that caused me to go in reverse and revisit my past. Naturally, people who had judged me before were in the front row to say, "I told you he wouldn't change." Realize that when you get in unfamiliar territory it may take some practice before you get it right, which isn't the end of the world—it is simply what it is. Eventually, you will find your way and regain control of your life if you are unrelenting. Time changes everything, and with persistence, we can keep the passion that fuels us reasonably unvarying. If we can just hold on long enough, time will, at last, create for us conditions in which we can succeed and make a difference.

NAVIGATE THE DETOURS

As you *Enjoy The Ride,*™ never forget that your personal and professional journey will always have some detours. Many people who dream of living a successful life never do because they are unwilling to change or follow direction. The ultimate outcome of anyone's life is a matter of personal choice. Our thought process is the power behind whether or not we will permit our lives to be motivated by a purpose. To be purpose-driven, you have to believe in yourself, be true to yourself, grow yourself, take responsibility for yourself, refocus yourself and change yourself.

When you are at the lowest point in your life, and everyone has abandoned belief in you, never stop believing in yourself. When you *believe in yourself,* you are better able to focus on improving.

When you don't believe in yourself, you expect the worst not only of yourself but of others.

If you are insecure, you struggle to center on anything but yourself because you are always worried about how you look, what others think about you and whether you're going to fail. Stop worrying about what other people think of you. Why is their opinion of you more important than your own? You will always be restricted when your future depends on the validation of others. Remember this: if you are afraid of criticism, you will depart this life doing nothing.

Be true to yourself. When the potholes of life materialize, search for a resolution and fuel your passion to keep the fire burning. Becoming defensive and hunting for a getaway plan reveals that your passion was not genuine. If you are looking for the conditions of any situation to be exactly right, you will struggle to be happy or successful. No matter what the circumstances, positive people see opportunities everywhere. They understand that opportunities aren't based on luck or position. They are realized by preparation and a positive attitude. Unearthing problems doesn't take anything special. What *is* exceptional, however, is seeing a solution for every problem and a possibility in every difficulty. Opportunity exists where you find it and always looks bigger going than coming.

It is also essential to surround yourself with people who have negotiated the detours of life and found opportunities in them. *Grow yourself* by finding a wise person who has accomplished what you wish for in your life and then apply it. Stop rationalizing your actions and pay attention to what they do.

Accepting instruction from people is a life-changing choice that will help you break away from your own negative thinking and allow you to grow.

Anytime you put up with mediocrity in your choice of acquaintances you become more comfortable with mediocrity in your life. Only a fool ignores the leadership of wise people. Charlie "Tremendous" Jones said, "The only difference between who you are today and the person you will be in five years will come from the books you read and the people you associate with."

Success is limited to individuals who understand and accept that they are in situations of their choosing. If your tendency is to say, "It's not my fault," and blame everyone but yourself, the probability of you ever being truly happy and successful is slight. You will forever have a reason or excuse for your current situation and, as expected, you will never see it as your responsibility. Unsuccessful people duck responsibility. Positive and successful people *take* responsibility for their lives. Your thinking dictates your decisions. Until you accept complete responsibility for your past, you will never be free to move into a brighter future. Allowing your spouse, friends and family to rationalize your behavior will only add to the difficulty. Accept responsibility for your problems—it is the beginning of wisdom. Who you are, where you are and where you will go are your responsibility—so take it!

Think about your situation. Have you ever been wronged? Have there been times when you haven't gotten everything you deserved? Do you spend your time and energy on what should have been, or are you going to focus on what can be? Even when truth and justice are on your side, you may never be able to right your wrongs. A major detour in your journey is when you allow destructive emotions to consume your energy and make you negative. As you look backward, trying to right your wrongs, you become resentful, angry, hateful and bitter. Instead of worrying about someone ever making it right, *refocus yourself* so you can move forward. Every mistake, broken promise and slip-up can develop a paralyzing grip. Stop wasting valuable hours envisioning revenge toward an uncaring person. Resentment is about another person who seldom gives thought to their offense. When you grant forgiveness, you release your past and create a new beginning. You can't make any progress when you are going the wrong way. If you want to get around the detours faster, then travel light. Remove all resentment, jealousies, self-centeredness and misgivings from your backpack.

> **A major diversion in your journey is when you allow destructive emotions to consume your energy and make you negative.**

You may not possess the ability to always make right decisions; however, you do hold the ability to make a decision and then make it right. You can change your future by *changing yourself*. Change requires action. It all comes down to this: There will come a time in your life when you will face a detour, and a decision is required. That decision, and how you make it, will have a far-reaching effect on generations unborn. Happiness and success are not the same for everyone because the meaning is different for every person. But the ultimate outcome of anyone's life will always be determined by their ability to navigate the detours.

MAKE THEM WONDER

One week after celebrating my fortieth birthday, my world would never be the same. I soon discovered there is no loneliness greater than the loneliness of a failure. With the exception of one person, every friend I had abandoned me when I needed them most. My wrong choices would lead to a divorce, loss of employment, humiliation and the forfeiture of financial health. Alone, unemployed, embarrassed and broke, I had three choices. Either let it define me, destroy me or strengthen me.

I am forever thankful to that one friend who said, "Your world is not over! Although you believe everything is finished, this is only beginning. *Stay strong and make them wonder how you're still smiling.*" That concluding sentence, containing ten words, would be the drive I needed for my wrong choice to strengthen me.

THE PARADOX OF
WRONG CHOICES

Sometimes the wrong choices bring us to the right places. For me, my test became my *test*-imony, and my mess became my *mess*-age. However, to reach the right place, it is a matter of objectively reviewing the conclusions you have drawn about life and recognizing that if they are not working *for* you, they are working *against* you. Instead of squandering time being angry about the circumstances you're in, be curious about how you got there. The truth is, if you would invest as much time and energy discovering what you did wrong (you're not faultless in the situation) as blaming everything on someone else, you would rapidly realize the condition you are in is of your own choosing. Until you accept responsibility for your past, stop trying to get even, and stop blaming your present circumstance on everyone but yourself. You will never control your future—history will. You can become better tomorrow than you are today, but it requires letting go of your past and learning from both success and failure. Letting go is painful. Growth is painful, but nothing is as painful as staying stuck somewhere you don't belong. It's time to *Turn The Page*!

KEEP LOOKING FORWARD

Only a fool trips over that which is behind him. We can engage in life and thrive today if we stop inviting the past into our present. The past can provide an object lesson. Past experiences can fill us with self-belief and the confidence to overcome a condition. They can also provide the impetus to move forward from the strength of previous accomplishments and hard-won achievements.

We can all learn from the lessons of history. History is one of the great teachers in life—that's why its study is so rewarding. If knowledge carries with it an obligation to act, then we must learn, adapt and adjust according to the lessons of the past.

If we permit the skeletons of yesterday to control today, we will prejudice our present and foreclose the future.

The choice is ours; we can make a decision every day to start anew in the thoughts we think and the actions that follow. No one I know wants to have dinner with the skeletons of the past pouring the wine and serving the food. We need to remind ourselves not to penalize all people for the transgressions of some. It's a tough one, I know, but think about it… "Dinner for two" doesn't need to be "dinner for twenty-two"… It's emotionally expensive and intellectually draining!

When I wrote my book *Enjoy The Ride*, I made the observation that life provides every opportunity to get it right. We can start over. If we have failed, we can always try again.

As I write these words yet again, my suspicion is that some of you might be thinking, "Oh, that's easy for you to say Steve, but I've messed up so many opportunities and lost so much time that I sometimes feel like it's useless."

I don't believe for a single minute that your life is hopeless! Yes, we can all get knocked down and knocked around and indeed we can encounter roadblocks, but that should never mean we cannot strive to have a sense of inner peace and greater accomplishment than we've previously known. If we have made mistakes in the past, we can learn from them and achieve a higher sense of balance to avoid missing our next opportunity.

WHEN YOU ARE IN THE WRONG STORY, LEAVE

Just because the past didn't turn out like you wanted it to, doesn't mean your future can't be better than you ever imagined. It's time to write the sequel that you want.

While it is true that the time we have lost cannot be replaced, and also true that we cannot travel back in time to do things over, I firmly believe it is never too late to pursue new opportunities no matter how modest or grand they may seem.

Moving on isn't about never looking back. It's about taking a glance at yesterday and noticing how much you've grown up since then.

At age 40 I turned the page and commenced writing a new story. I began to recognize that you become strong when you know your weakness. You become beautiful when you finally see your flaws. You become wise when you learn from your mistakes. You begin laughing more because you've faced sadness, and you can love again because you have known animosity.

The past is a place of reference, not a place of residence. There is only one way to live the story you want to tell: *Turn the Page!*

▶

TO HAVE
STEVE
SPEAK AT YOUR
NEXT EVENT...

CALL
866-445-5452
724-540-5019

EMAIL
bookings@stevegilliland.com

VISIT
www.stevegilliland.com

STEVE *Gilliland*
HALL OF FAME SPEAKER